THE LONG

AND

SHORT

OF IT

by Cheryl Nathan and Lisa McCourt
illustrated by Cheryl Nathan

Troll
BridgeWater Paperback

To Lisa McCourt, for making so much possible — C.N.

To GVC, who knows the shortest route to my long-on-love heart — L.M.

Text copyright © 1998 by Cheryl Nathan and Lisa McCourt.
Illustrations copyright © 1998 by Cheryl Nathan.

Published by BridgeWater Paperback, an imprint and trademark
of Troll Communications L.L.C.

First published in hardcover by BridgeWater Books.

First paperback edition published 1999.

Produced by Boingo Books, Inc.

Printed in the United States of America.

10 9 8 7 6 5 4 3 2 1

Library of Congress Cataloging-in-Publication Data

Nathan, Cheryl, 1958-
The long and short of it / by Cheryl Nathan and Lisa McCourt; illustrated by Cheryl Nathan.
p.   cm.
Summary: Uses different animals to introduce the concept of size, comparing,
for example, the length of a ring-tailed lemur's tail with that of a Boston terrier.
ISBN 0-8167-4545-5 (lib. bdg.)   ISBN 0-8167-5609-0 (pbk.)
1. Size perception—Juvenile literature. [1. Size.   2. Animals.]
I. McCourt, Lisa.   II. Title.
BF299.S5N37   1998
152.14'2—dc21   97-33064

No two animals are alike.
Some have long
parts and some have
short parts, but their
differences are what
make them special.

Take the ring-tailed lemur, for instance. Its tail is longer than a skateboard.

But a Boston terrier's tail is shorter than a half-used black crayon.

And who can grow its beak longe

A chicken has a bea

Its beak is as short as a grape

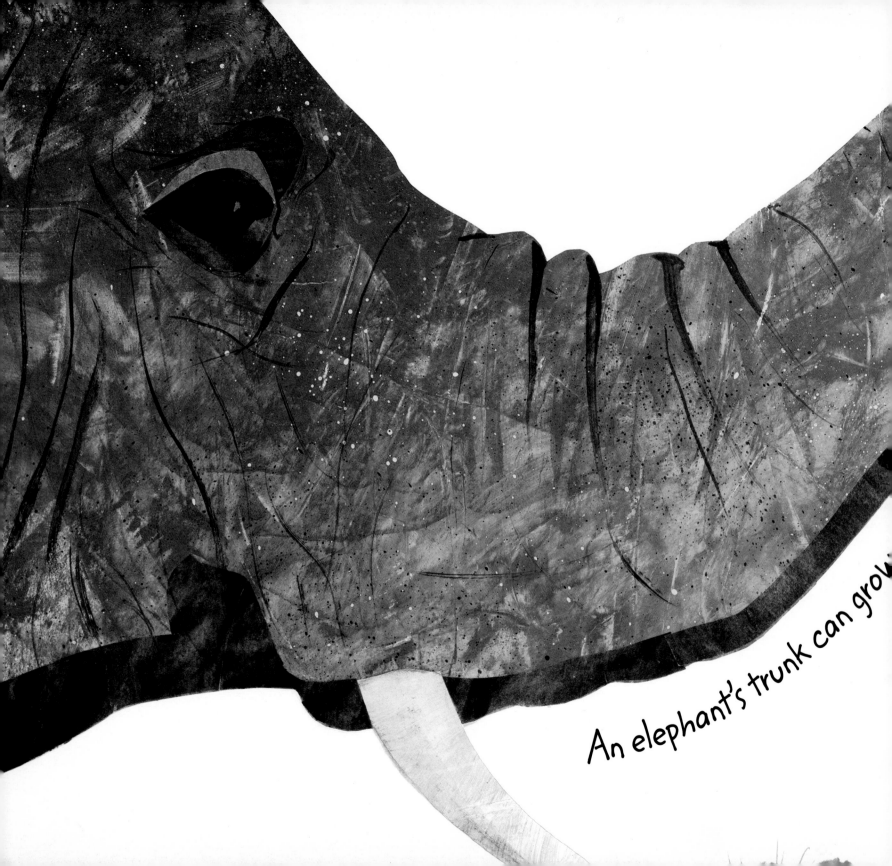

An elephant's trunk can grow

longer than a car trunk—even longer than some whole cars! But I bet you don't know about the other animal that has a trunk. It's the tiny elephant shrew, with a trunk as short as a broken toothpick.

A giraffe makes a good friend because it'll really stick its neck out.

for you—and its neck is as long as your bedroom door!

Zebras' necks are shorter than chair legs.

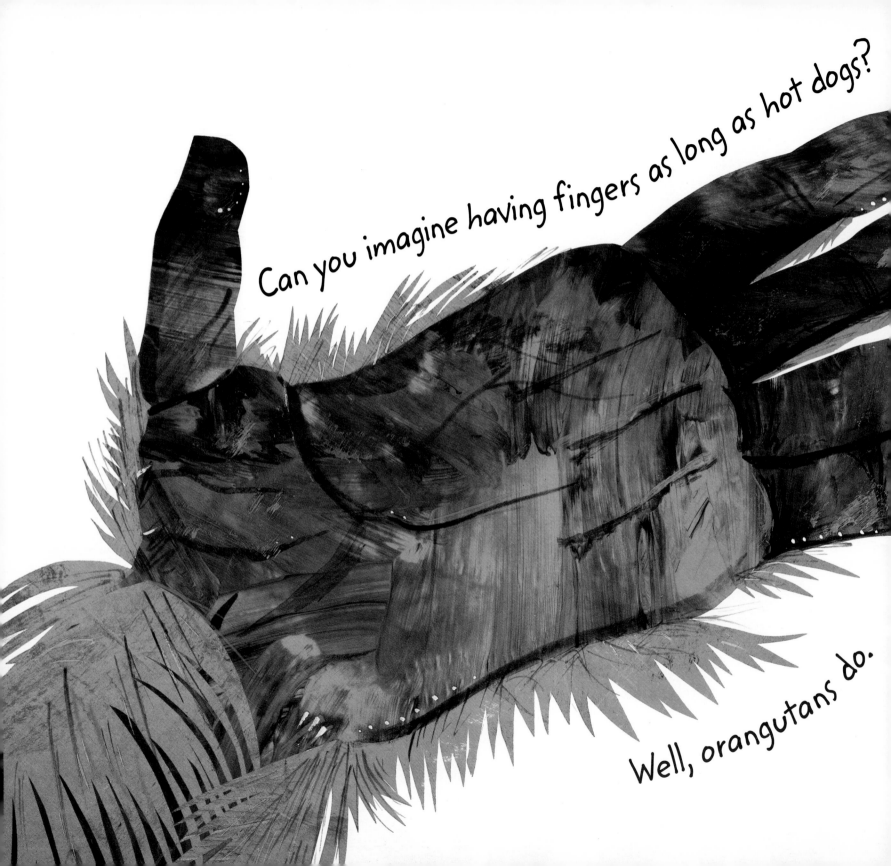

But the giant panda's little fingers are shorter than yo-yos.

Reindeer have long antlers— longer than your arms stretched out as **wide** as you can **stretch** them.

Mountain goats' horns are
as short as carrots.

Could you fit an aardvark's snout in your lunch box?

Nope! Too long! (And why would you want to, anyway?)

Hippos are big,

but their ears are little— about as short as Ping-Pong balls.

Hares are little animals with long ears —almost as long as tissue boxes.

Peacock feathers are as long as jump ropes—

but not as much fun to play with. The feathers on top of a cockatiel's head are as short as inchworms.

The longest hair a person ever grew was almost fourteen feet—as long as a seesaw!

The little hairs on the top of a mangabey monkey's head are shorter than the bristles on your toothbrush.

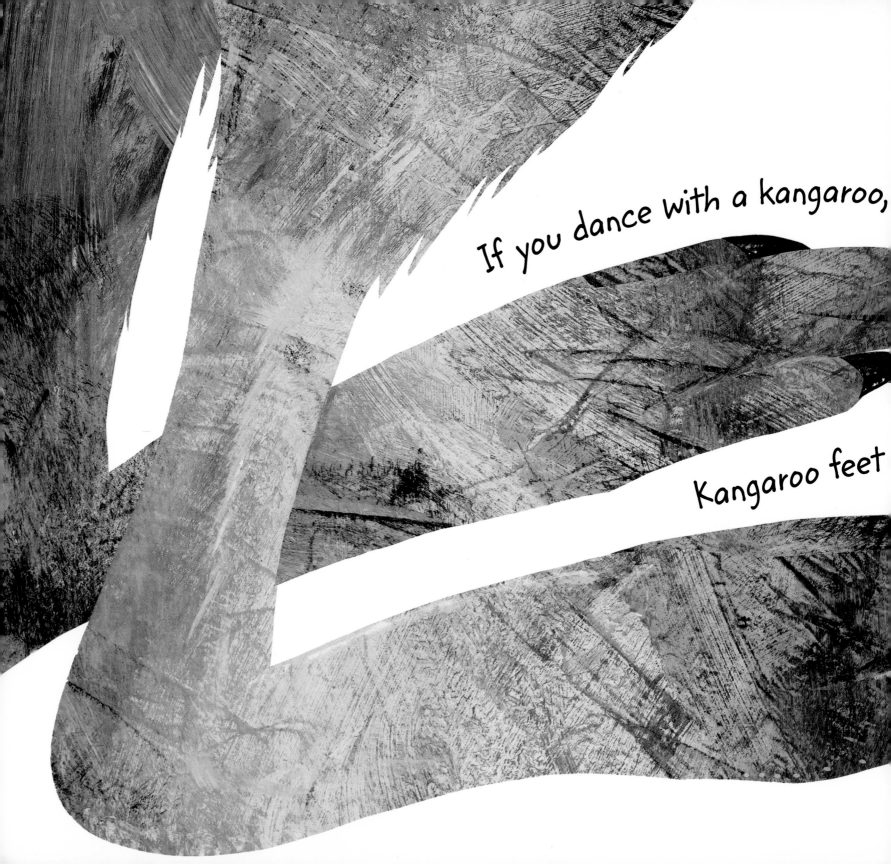

If you dance with a kangaroo,

Kangaroo feet

don't let it step on your toes!

are longer than whole watermelons.

Your foot is probably shorter than a carton of milk.

If you had lived in prehistoric days, you'd have seen huge woolly mammoths running through your backyard. Their tusks were as long as playground slides, and even more curvy.

Some walrus tusks are as short as drinking straws.

Don't stick out your tongue at a chameleon! Its tongue is as long as its whole body—

A raccoon's little tongue is as short as a stick of gum.

and that's longer than a fire hydrant.

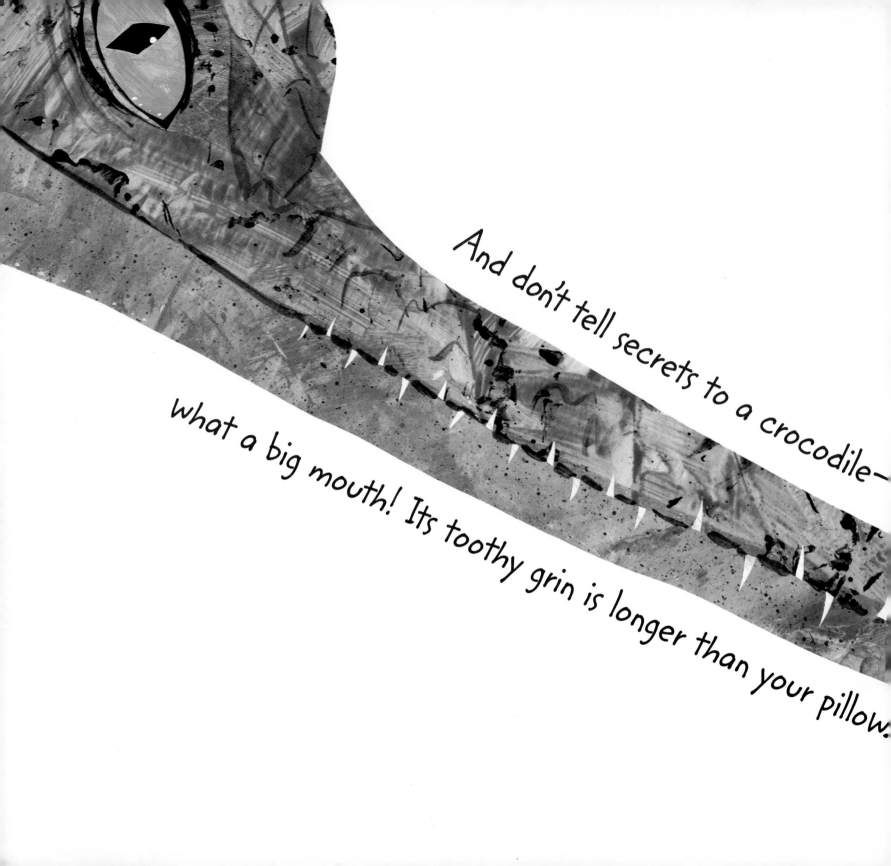

And don't tell secrets to a crocodile—

what a big mouth! Its toothy grin is longer than your pillow.

But this bottle-nosed dolphin's mouth is as short as a pencil.

If you look for them,
you'll find long parts and
short parts everywhere—

and that's the
long and short of it!